EDUCATIONAL ROBOT

JOHN LOK

Contents

Preface

Introduction

Nowadays, artificial intelligent technology and online technology and online book stores are high technological intelligent product. Hence, human ourselves will have possible to cause artificial intelligent machine men to own human's mind to learn how to read books and/or write books abilities. When artificial intelligent machine men can learn how to read books and/or write books. Consequently, it means that artificial intelligent machine men can own human mind to do any jobs.

This book aims to explain how to apply artificial intelligent education machine to teach students in schools. If one day, artificial intelligent machine men can be invent to own human's mind and judgement abilities. I believe that universities can attempt to apply artificial intelligent machine men to teach students in lecturer hall. When, artificial intelligent machine men can be invented to learn how to reading any books, writing any books, learning any subject knowledge, even learn how to make judgement to answer any students studying challenges. Then, it is possible that they can be applied to replace universities lecturers their teaching jobs to teach students in univeristy hall.

I suppose artificial intelligent technology will be one popular new technological education method to replace university lecturers to teach their students in university lectuer hall in the future. When the human lecturer teach whose subjects knowledge to let the artificial intelligent machine man to learn and to remember what every univeristy course content that the human lecturer will speak in univeristy teaching hall. Then, the artificial intelligent machine man can replace the human lecturer to attempt to teach whose subject students in univeristy lecturing hall. So, if the artificial intelligent machine leactuer is invented to own human's mind and judgement and analyzing abilities, then it can attempt to analyze every student's enquiries concerning every time lecturing content questions in order to answer their enquires. Due to they had learnt the course content to remember to their artificial intelligent brain, so it is possible that they can answer any student's enquires suddenly in lecturing halls.

In my this book, I shall assume when artificial intelligent machine men can learn how to write books and/ or read books. Then, they will have human's mind ability in possible. Can future artificial intelligent machine men be invented to learn how to write books and/or read books ability? In my this book, I shall attempt to answer this question. Finally, I hope my readers can attempt to make judgement whether artificial intelligent machine men can really learn how to write and read books to do lecturer's teaching job.

In the future, AI technology can be applied to education industry. It will be one new technological popular education tool to assist university teachers to teach their students after the human lecturers had taught their teaching subject contents to let them to remember before every time lecturing teaching in lecture hall. To explain how AI technological technology can be apply to developing countries in Asia, e.g. Philippines, Korea, China, US, UK etc. developed countries to replace human lecturers to teach their students popularly. The benefits of AI machine teaching lecturer can assist human lecturer to teach students in lecturing halls, then human lecturers can concentrate on researching jobs.

Prologue

Table of contents

1

Artificial intelligence and the future of defense or teaching choice

Nowadays, artificial intelligence (AI) is widely knowledge to be one kind of the dramatic technology. However, it is expected to continue, to have a disruptive impact on human's private and public life, so defense and security will be no exception. But how exactly will these be affected ? How will (AI) defense and security is incremental in nature? If (AI) technological machine men are applied to teach students in education aspect, is it better to my next generation learning develpment more than they are applied to war attack aspect.

To research why artificial intelligence (AI) has possible to be used to cause autonomous weapons by human. We need to understand these three aspects of relationship. They include cybersecurity and artificial intelligence and machine learning and autonomous weapon systems relationship between of them. Basic on (AI) machine can be invented to learn any new knowledge, so if (AI) machine men are taught how to attack enemy, which will be such as human soldier function. But, if (AI) machine men are taught how to learn university knowledge to teach students. Then, they will be such as human lecturer function. So, when (AI) is invented to own human mind and judgement and learning abilities, then they will be either human's enemy or human's assistant, such as university lecturer's assistant.

Firstly, we need to know what is the mean of artificial intelligence and cyber defense/offense? It means defense of critical networks: real time, pattern finding, anomaly seeking, it must utilize machine (AI) learning algorithms to efficiently, and instantaneously respond to potential network threats as well as it means human on or out of the loop. On the loop : it means anomaly detection: human notified, IT analysis, response. Out of the loop: it means anomaly detection: (AI) decides best method of response: quarantine, honey pot monitoring, hack-back. Thus, it is possible that (AI) can be used , such as autonomous cyber weapon. If (AI) is applied to make the decision best method of response to learning aspect, such as univeristy different subject knowledge. Then, it will be one good technological educational tool to teach university students.

In simplicity, (AI) can be one of scientific weapons platform or one of university teaching tool. When one day, it is invented to be applied to control war planes to fly to any countries to attack enemies or it is invented to be seemed to human to replace soldiers to bring guns or any weapons go to other countries to attack. So, it is possible that future any war defense planes, (AI) technological automatic control weapon can be replaced of human soldiers or war plane pilots to control any war defense planes to go to different enemy countries to attack them easily. It is very horror matter to threaten global human's ourselves life in the future , if (AI) automatic control war defense planes or (AI) automatic control machine soldiers were invented successfully. Otherwise, when one day, (AI) machine lecturer is invented to be applied to learn university different subjects knowledge to replace lecturers to copy lecturer's every prepared lecturer course to speak to let students to listen when they are sitting in university halls as well as the (AI) machine lecturer can make analysis and judgement response to answer every student's enquire immedicately after it had speaking all courses to students to listen in lecturer hall every time. Then, it can let human lecturer does any education job duty, e.g. research education work. So, (AI) machine lecturer will be future human lecturer's assistant in future one day.

Finally, the most serious (AI) technological invention risks are human is unknown these aspects of (AI) absolutely: They are not simple automatic systems, learning reasoning, communication of " self-aware" systems. Thus, human will face (AI) technological invention risks or threats if human invent (AI) machine man to learn how to attack enemy. Otherwise, if human invent (AI) machine man to learn how to teach univerity student. I believe that my future university students can raise learn ability and writing ability and reading ability from (AI) machine lecturer teaching more than human lecturer teaching.

1.1 Online technology and online book technology influences artificial intelligence mind development

Nowadays, online technological invention bring online book technological development. Also, artificial intelligent technological machine men had been invented to link internet to do any jobs, e.g. children can find any data from artificial intelligent machine men when the artificial intelligent machine man had been installed internet and computer function, then children can find any online books to read from the artificial intelligent machine man. Such as Japan artificial intellgent machine men had installed computer and internet function, the Japan family children can find any online books to read from the artificial intelligent machine man at Japan any families' homes conveniently. Hence, it implies that future one day, artificial intelligent machine has possible to be invented to own human's reading and/or writing abilities.

For example,online book publishing is one kind of popular internet technology. For example, Amazon publish is as a business model with many potential advantages, relative to a physical operation. It held out the potential of lower book inventing and distribution costs and reduced overhead. Consumers could find the books, they were looking for more easily and a variety book topic choices could be offered for sale. It can accept and fulfill orders from almost any domestic location with equal ease. And most purchasers made on its site would be exempt from sales tax. One Amazon strategy hand, it would have to make its returns and redress processes transparent and reliable, and offer other ways for clients to learn, as much about the book possible before buying. Future online book market development trend, such as Amazon, Barnes & Noble etc. online book shops.

Hence, online book store technology can be applied to artificial intelligent technology. Such as artificial intelligent machine men can apply computer technology to learn the abilities of reading and/or writing any books either on paper or on computer. Hence, it is possible that artificial intelligent machine men will have similar human's writing and/or reading books ability when they own human's mind ability. However, it bring this questions: Can artificial intelligent machine men own human's mind abilities? If they own human's mind abilities, is it mean that they can write and/or read any books? Can artificial intelligent machine men own human's mind abilities to create to write any books? Can artificial intelligent machine men own human's mind abilities to read and make any judgements or decisions more accurate than human's judgements or decisions? To answer these questions? I shall indicate that online book reading and writing technology can be applied to artificial intelligent machine men reading and writing technology. Because they are similiar computer mind technological development. So, I believe that future artificial intelligence machine men can be invented to own similar human's reading and writing's mind abilities in future one day.

I believe artificial intelligence and online technological reading abilities are very similiar. Nowadays, computer can be invented to attempt to read and write any books by human. Why can not artificial intelligent machine men replace computer to read and write any books? Artificial intelligent machine men can replace human to attempt to write or/and read books, due to artificial intelligent machine men had invented to own human mind to do some jobs and their mind had been invented to be similiar to human behavioral abilities to do these behaviors, e.g. cooking, driving, playing games, singing songs, speaking, listening, frighting etc. different human's abilities. So, it seems that artificial intelligent will be possible to be invented to own human's mind abilities to do any writing or reading behaviors or functions.

1.2 Prediction of artificial intelligence reading and writing abilities

development

What is future trend of artificial intelligence reading and writing abilities development? To answer this question, we need to know what benefits of artificial intelligent machine men can attribute to human's needs when they can own any human's mind to read or/and write any books.

I shall indicate e-books reading and writing example, if artificial intelligent machine men can be invented to own human's mind to write and/or read e-books on computer. Then, it brings this question: Can artificial intelligent machine men assist human to learn to do judgement to solve any challenges?

I believe that when artificial intelligent machine men can be invented to own human mind to write or/and read any books, then they will own human's mind ability to make judgement to solve any challenges more accurately, even their decisions can be more accurate to compare to human's decisions. So, artificial intelligent machine mens' writing and reading ability is the main factor to cause their mind to do any judgement in order to make any decisions more accurately. Consequently, in future one day, artificial intelligent machine mens' writing and reading ability will be invented to similar human's reading and writing abilities as well as their minds can also be invented to similar human's minds as well as their judgement abilities can be invented to similar to human's judgement abilities to make any decisions more accurate.

1.3 The influences when AI is invented to own human's mind and judgement abilities

Finally, I shall discuss what are the influences when AI is invented to own human's mind and judgement abilities in our future job market. The achievement of artificial intelligent (AI) machine men achievement requirement of owning human's mind and judgement abilities which requires extensive manual labor, and by augmenting the calling process with machine learning, the process where speed and accuracy are needed to close to human's mind and judgement abilities. Expert human race callers now have better information at artificial intelligent machine men at their fingertips faster.

Hence, if the above those requirements are achieved to satisfy artificial intelligent machine men ind and judgement abilities demand to close or exceed humans' mind and judgement abilities. Then, I believe that future human's some simple jobs must be replaced by (AI) machine men. Even, human's some professonal jobs, e.g. lawyer, accountant, administator, typing etc. professional skillful jobs, which will be either replaced or will be assisted by (AI) machine men. For example, (AI) machine men learn how to type english or other language words to do typing job ; they can learn how to apply accounting knowledge to record any firm's income and expenditure record of accounting job; they can also learn how to assist architects to design any architectural building drawing plans to do architect jobs; they can learn how to analyze any court evidences to judge any criminal or civil cases and assist lawyers to give legal advices to achieve more reasonable judgement for any legal cases; they can also learn how to assist firm's managers or administrators to manage any organization teams efficiently.

Consequently, when (AI) machine men can be invented to achieve to exceed human's mind and judgement abilities level. Then, I believe that they can do instead of human' simple jobs, which can do even human's more difficult and more judgement requirement of professional skillful jobs. So, (AI) machine men must need to achieve to do any jobs, they are same, even exceed to human professionals' abilities. Then, it will cause a lot of human's jobs to be disappeared or some human's jobs will be replaced by owning judgement and mind abilities of (AI) machine men to do.

Hence, future many human's jobs will be replaced by technological labors. Employers choose to buy (AI) machine men to replace human labors. The reasons include (AI) machine men have none unhappy, angry emotin to influence their low efficiencies and low productivities. Their judgement and mind abilities can exceed human's abilities or do any jobs to compare better performance to human's abilities. Consequently, different occupation labors need to prepare to learn how to co-operate with (AI) machine men to let future employers feel (AI) machine men will be human's assistant to assist human to do jobs efficiently when human and (AI) machine men work together. It aims to avoid future employers feel (AI) machine men's judgement and mind abilities can exceed any low knowledgeable and skilful occupation labors, even high knowledge and skilful occupation labors. It means that (AI) machine men are only labors' assistant if (AI) machine mens' judgement and mind abilities are below under to human labors' judgement and mind abilities.

Consequently, to avoid (AI) machine men can replace human to do any simple or complex jobs to cause any future any occupation labors' competitiors. I recommend that it is right time labors ought prepare to learn different skills. So, every individual labor does not only concentrate on one kind of skill. Because supposing one kind of the occupation labor's job duties are replaced by (AI) machine men. If the employee had owned more than one kind of occupation skill. Then, I believe that who can avoid the unemployment threat more easier than the employee only owned one kind of occupation skill, when (AI) machine men had invented to own human's mind and judgement abilities in future one day.

2

Why educational robot can raise education quality

When (AI) machine men can own human reading and writing and judgement and analytical abilities, then they can replace university lecturers to teach students to raise students‘ learning abilities absolutely. Then, it bring this question: Why does I machine lecturer can raise education quality? Why do universities prefer to apply (AI) machine lecturer to teach teachers more than human lectuer in university lecturer hall learning environment? Will (AI) university lecturers replace human lecturers to teach students to learn at university lecturing halls popularly? Can (AI) university lecturers replace university human lecturers to teach students more easily and it can let students feel more easily to learn when they are listening what (AI) university lecturers are teaching to them every time university lecture.

In university today, nearly all students need to attend university lecturing hall to listen their lecturer's teaching in every time course. However, many students do not feel interesting to attend university halls to listen human lecturer's teaching. The reasons include, they are busy, so no time to attend lecturer's hall to listen lecturer's teaching; or they feel bore to listen their lecturer's teaching; they feel difficulty to learn; they have confidence to exam and do their assignments, so they feel that they do not need to go to lecturing halls to listen their human lecturer's teaching. However, if one day, (AI) machine lecturers are invented to teach university students to learn and solve their learning difficulties. Can it raise student individual learning interest, due to (AI) machine lecturers' education quality is better than human lecturers' education quality?

What will influence to university students if (AI) machine lecturer can invented to replace human lecture? The influences will include such as below:

First reason: the only way is going to be useful to university lecturers are if all (AI) machine lecturers are well-informed and fully supported to assist human lectuers to teach whose students to let them to listen whose teaching absolutely. So, human lecturers can concentrate on doing any education research and data gathering jobs to prepare for (AI) machine lecturers to help them to explain human lecturers' every time prepared course contents more efficiently. So, (AI) machine lectuers can help human lecturers to share whose teaching time in lecturing halls. Human lecturers' can spend whose hall lecturing time to do whose educational research or other educational gathering jobs absolutely.

The second reason, the human lecturer (Human capital) has ability and efficiency of concentrating on education data gatehering research jobs to prepare to write whose books. When (AI) machine lecturer replace the human lecturer to spend time to attend lecturing hall to teach students. Fo long term, the human lecturer can raise education productivity growth and education quality raising, due to who only concentrate on searching or gathering data to prepare to write whose books to raise their education level.

In macro and micro economic view, the well (AI) machine lecturer educated labor (human capital) is often replaced to human lecturer as one of the critical factors to influence rapid education productivities and educational quality growth to the Asia developing countries' any regions or cities. Because any of these Asia developing countries, such as China, Korea, Philippines etc. countries which need have well educated and knowledgeable lecturer labors to raise any universities' educational productivities and educational qualities growth. So (AI) assistant lecturer factors which ought have close relationship to cause the good or bad future student learning effectiveness and education or learning qualities raising in these any one of Asia developing countries.

The third reason, for the big population of student growth number example, China's student growth rate is larger than school growth rate. If China expect every students have enough chance to study in schools, but university human lectuer numbers are not enough to supply to universities to teach their students. I believe that (AI) machine lecturer is only one kind of teaching method to solve these big population countries' university lectuer number shortage challenge.

In conclusion, in long term, (AI) machine lecturers can solve university human lecturer shortage challenge as well as they can attract many students to attend lecturing halls and human lecturers can raise education quality when they can concentrate on searching or gathering data to prepare their education career, when (AI) machine lectuers replace them to spend time to attend univesity halls to teach students in every university lecturing time.

3

Future educational robot market development

4

Learning educational robot influences human behavior

Human Behavioral network job brings social economic benefits

What does human network job mean ? Why may human network job be popular? Why human network job behavior may influence economy ?

Nowadays internet is popular to use. We can apply internet to find data , search any new things, even earn money. Why does internet

may become huma network job source. For example, e-publish may be one kind of new human network job. Any authors may apply internet

channel to help them to sell electronic or paper books from e-publisher web store. They may apply facebook, you tub etc. any online

channel to promote themselves new books to let new

readers to know whether when they may buy themselves favourable new topic books to read
from electronic publisher web store.

Thus, future electronic publisher industry may help any authors to build internet network platform to help them to sell and promote
ot advertise their any one new electronic or paper book topic to let global any one reader to choose to buy their any new topic books from electronic publisher web store easily and conveniently. However, it implies that electronic network platform author may be one kind of future new human network job in our societies.

How electronic network platform author job may bring economy benefit in macro economy view? A person can have few friends, contacts and still be very influential if these few
friends and contacts are themselves highly influential, e.g. one author must not need to know any one reader in global society. When they like to choose any electronic books from electronic internet network platform. They may become the author's any one topic book buyer, when they feel the author's any one topic book is fun and attract they make decision to buth the strange author whose the topic book from electronic book publisher's platform web store conventiently in short time. Although, they are strangers, they do not know themselves , but the reader can understand what it way that made Google from writing platofrm to create new creative mind and typing network job method to replace traditional hand writing book method for global authors. It will be one kind of new human network writing job.

Hence, global any one reader can apply an innovative search engine , such as google.com to find whether whom

author personal new topic books are value to read from internet.
Then, the electroniuc publisher's web store may be new book store platform sale network to help the author to sell many electronic or paper books from electronic network platform
in short time. So, internet may be future new network plaform to help global any one author to create network writing job absolutely. Furthermore, internet may be popular social media
to help any one author to build goold relationship between his/her readers. It is one kind of new network, human network job. New authors do not need to buy many paper books to prepare to put in any one book shop warehouse. Their every book can print on demand to reduce out of book stock in any one book shop. They may choose to sell either electronic books or paper books both from any one book publisher web store. So, electronic network platform may be one kind of good writing channel to help human authors to create income and it can also
help authors to bring new creative mind and new topic fun content books to let readers to know and buy to read from electronic publisher network platform.

Why does human behavior may be one kind of new human network job to bring global economic advantages. ALthough, it may be free income or without inocme, but the person does the network behavior, his/her behavior may be bring advantages to influence many other people's health. For this case, when a worker in a coffee shop in an airport gets a vaccination aganinst the flu, it does not only helps him or her stay healthy, but also helps the many travellers who might otherwise have been inflected if that workers caught the flu.

So, the externality , the result implies the vaccination of even a part of a community conveys benefits to the whole community. For example, governments pay special attention
to the vaccinations of school children, teachers, health mothers, and the elderly, categories of people particularly susceptible not only to catching, but also to transmitting a disease.

It is not accidental that governments are heavily involved with vaccination . When there are externalities, free market, fail to persuade individual incentives with society's
their the worker's decision of whether to get a vaccine ends up attracting whether other people get sick. The workers might not
fully take all these other people's potential suffering into account when making her or his vaccination decision.

As Stanford University does many suggestions, understand this and tries to help them make the right decisions and so providers free flu vaccines for its staff and students.

Small pockets of unvaccinated individuals can allow a disease to gain a spread more widely well-being. For example, parent weighing the costs and benefits of a vaccine for their child is not always thinking of the consequences of that vaccination to other people. THese are markets in which subsidizing or regulating behavior can make everyone better off. Because the reason for requiring that a child be vaccinated before enrolling in school is not just to protect that child, because each child's vaccination affects others via potential contagions.

Robots take our jobs behavioral and economy influences

Robot job behavior brings economy influences

If one day robots can replace human to do simple, even complex jobs. They will bring what influences to our global societial economy.The popular economic refrain declares that the

global middle class is dying and robots will soon take our jobs, e.g. shopping center customer service jobs, library service jobs, cinema ticket sale jobs, restaurant kitchen cooker jobs,

even, bus drivers, taxi drivers etc. public transport driving jobs, accountant, doctors etc. professional jobs. Whether it is beautiful or petty matter if our future societies have many human jobs can be replaced to do from robots. Businessman must may reduce to employ employees and reduce to pay salary or wage, when robots can be replaced to do their employees tasks. But, societies must bring unemployement rate rises , due to societies will have many people loss jobs when their employers choose to buy robots to serve their clients or do any office tasks or customer service or cleaning etc. tasks.

In micro economy view, employers may save money in long term, but in macro economy view, it will cause unemployment ratio rises , even crime rate rises when there are many people lose

jobs in societies. These models of doom, though, fail to account for the hundreds of businesses riding the waves of change in their industries when robots may be invented to replace human to do many simple , even complex tasks in our future societies.

WE may image that one small factory needs to manufacture fishes canes to sell to supermarket, the small , cheaper stuff and higher margin parts of the fishes manufacture industry. Before, this factory needs to employe many human factory workers need to help every fresh customer makeing the perfect fishing gear, designed for performance, durability, and cost in order to achieve to manufacture every fish cane in whole fished processing manufacturing stages. Every worker needs to spend about 15 to twenty minutes to finish every fish cane , till to delivery to any supermarket to sell. If this fish canes manufacturing factory can apply manufacturing robots to help them to finish any one working tasks , every robot can only spend five minutes to finish whole fresh fish cane manufacturing process. Thus, every robot can help this factory save 10 to 15 minutes time to finsh every fish cane manufacturing process. IN fact, time is money, because when every robot can help this factory to reduce 10 to 15 minutes time to compare human worker. Then, this factory can finish about 20 fish canes in one hour if it can use robot to help it to manufacture fish canes. Otherwise, if this factory still use human workers to help it to manufacture fish canes, then it can finsh about 3 to 4 fish canes in one hour. SO, the manufacturing efficiency ensures that robots must help this fish manufacturing factory to raise fish canes number more than human workers. So, in robotic behavioral economy view, manufacturing robots must help this fish canes manufacturing factory to raise fish canes manufacturing number and deliver increasing number to supermarkets to prepare to sell every day. Robots can help this fish canes manufacturing factory bring manufacturing time saving, rising manufacturing efficiency, improving performance and reducing wages expenditure long time advantages in micro economy view. However, manufacturing robots can also bring disadvanages to society, e.g. increasing unemployment ratio, increasing

crime rate,
this factory workers will lose jobs and income, they need earn social welfare from government and increasing government finance pressure in short time, even long time in macro economic view.

Stanford University graduate program in economics, Scott lecturer explained that "in demand and supply economic theory for robots supply and demand case, robots supply number increasing may influence human workers demand number decrease. It sometimes calls " the efficient frontier".

No specific human beings were mentioned in any of economics classes. As robots supply and demand in market case, They (robots) may be purely theoretical " agents" who reached to the most reasonable sale prices in order to persuade any one businessman buyer to make manufacturing robot buying decision whether robots can help him / her to bring how much saving time , saving money, saving cost, improving performance, efficiency economic benefit before he/she plans to reduce workers number when he/she decides to apply robots to replace human workers in his/her factory or office or any service department, e.g. cinema ticket sale service, shopping center customer service, shopping center cleaning , supermarket customer service etc. service or sale tasks. When robots can replace human to do any one of these tasks in any organizations. So, robots may be human worker agents who reached to prices the way robots would react to a software command. There was nothing that explained why some people thrived and others did n't or why truly brilliant, hardworking people could fail when much lazier folks succeeded." Having been admitted to the Stanford University graduate program in economics, Scott lecturer hoped to get his answers there.

How robots influence our future social changing? Using the right technology can be a boon to your business in this economy. For internet example, it is easier than ever to find well-matched customers
all around the world, to stay in contact with them, and to more quickly design the products they want. If you focus solely on being cutting -edge, though you risk letting the technology
take over what should be very robust relationships with your customers , employees, and colleagues. IN nowaddays society, technoligical advances and cutomation, personal relationships in business are more crucial than ever. I mean that robots can not replace human to serve clients to let them to feel more comfortable and passion more easily. For shoe shop case example, if the shoe shop apply one robot to serve its clients to replace human shoe salesperson to serve its shoe customers. Robots ensure that they can not persuade every shoe potential buyer to make shoe buying decision more easily when robots need to contact every shoe potential buyer. The reason is simple, because robots can not touch any one shoe buyer individual emotion very easier.

If the shoe buyer needs the robots to help him/her to choose any right shoe styles when he/she can not feel himself / herself can make the most right shoe style choice decision. The robots can not replace human shoe salesperson to make shoe style choice judgement more easily. They must need longer time to analyze whether which shoe style may be the most suitable to the shoe buyer. Otherwise,human shoe salesperson may attempt to make the most right shoe style choice decision to help any one shoe buyer to chooce the most right style shoe because he/

she owns shoe style sale experience, shoe style knowledge, the most important reason is that they can feel every shoe customer individual emotion to touch whether he/she will feel comfortable or happy when they attempt to help every shoe customer to seek the most right shoe style in every shoe customer whole shoe searching processing. Othwerwise, serving robots are only one machine, they can not touch or feel every shoe customer individual emotion whether he/she feel comfortable or unhappy or happy when they need to contact them in whole shoe searching processing. Hence, I believe that some tasks robots can not repalce human staff to do very easily. Otherwise, robots may bring disadvanatges to let any one businessman to loss his/her customers, due to robots can not touch every customer
emotion to compare human staff in service tasks more easily. Robots serving customer behaviors may cause money lose and customers number lose to the shop in micro economic view.

Intellectual human economic behaviors

What does intellectual human economic behaviors mean ? I believe that when we choose or decide to do intellectual behaviors, then our societies will be influenced to bring economic growth in consequence.I shall attempt to indicate pollution case to explain how and why eithet our intellectual or foolish behaviors may bring economic growth or recession in consequence as below:

On one hand, for air pollution social case aspect example, if we only consider to buy cars to drive for working aimr or holiday leisure aim. Then, our societies air will be polluted. Our health will be influenced to bad. Our car driving behaviors may cause global environment air pollution serously. In long tiem, global air pollution will bring our bodies health to be bad. Although, ourselves car driving behaviors may bring our driving travelling leisure enjoyment and comfortable feeling in short time, also we so not need to pay public transport fare often, but we need to compensate ourselves health economic intangible loss due to air pollution , when cars number increases, dirty air will cause ouselves health to become bad.

In the result, we will need to pay more medical expenditure when we are old age, due to ourselves bodies will become bad, due to we breathe global dirty air every day, due to ourselves cars pollute air in long time, e.g. 10 to 20 years, even 30 more without limited air pollution environment. So, driving cars behavior may be one kind of human foolish behavior and our foolish behavior may bring ourselves future long time medical expenditure absolutely.

One the other hand, water pollution social aspect, if we often keep much rubblish to pollute sea, oil exploration porcessing pollute ocean , ships gas pollute ocaen, then fishes will eat polluted food and drive dirty water, due to global ocean is polluted.

In fact, because human only to conside how to buy boats to carry on leisure enjoyment activities, or catch cruises to travel on the sea. Also, oil manufacturers only consider researching anywhere to find new oil exploration places to manufacture oil product, when their oil exploration processes pollute ocarn . Consequently, global fishes drink polluted warer or eat polluted food. They will have poison. SO, human will have high chance to eat poison polluted fishes, due to fishes are poison or are polluted.

So, human is doing foolish activities, we only hope to find oil exploration places to pollute ocean or we only spend money to buy ticket to catch ships to travel anywhere in global ocean. All of these human foolish behaviors will bring pollution to global ocean. On consequently, we will need to compensate to eat polluted or dirty or poision fishes, ourselves bodies health will be bad. In long time, we need have high chance to pay medical expenditure when we are old. So, pollution case may be one good example to explain how and why human foolish behavior may influence ourselves future need to compensate serious medical loss.

All of these human foolish behavior will bring pollution to global ocean. On consequently, we will need to compensate to eat polluted or dirty or poison fished , ourselves bodies health will be bad. In long time, we will have high chance to pay medical expenditure, when we are old. So, pollution case may be one good example to explain how and why human ourselves intellectual or foolish behaviors may influence future long time economic loss or economic growth or recession in micro and micro economic view.

On another water pollution aspect hand, if we often keep rubbish to sea, oil exploration processing pollutes ocean and ships' gas pollute ocean, then fishes will eat polluted food and drink dirty water, due to fishes will eat polluted food and drink dirty sea water because the global ocean is polluted seriously.

In fact, because human only consider how to buy boats to carry on any leisure water activities, or catches cruises to travel on the sea. Also, oil manufacturers only consider any where to find oil exploratin places to manufacture oil products from ocean, when their pol exploration processes can plooute ocean. Consequently, global fishes drink polluted water or eat direty food. They will have poison. So, human will have high chance to eat poison fishes.

Otherwise, such as pollution case, it can infuence inflation or deflation. Consequently, the reason indicates supply and demand theory. If air pollution is serious, then we will consider health issue, global cars demand number may be influenced to reduce, when global cars number demand will reduce, global car prices and supply number will need to change to fall down in order to attract or persuade global car consumers choose to make car purchase decision.

Hence, global car manufacture number and car price will be influenced to reduce, due to global air pollution issue. Consequently, deflation will occur because when the country citizen usually does not spend much extra saving money to buy car expensive goods. Money value will be low.

Otherwise, if global cair pollution is not serious, human considers to buy cars to enjoy driving leisure lives. So, global car demand is influenced to increase , also global car price will also influenced to increase.

Consequently, gobal human will choose to buy cars to drive. Due to we accept to spend extra saving to buy expensive car goods. Car sale price and supply may be influenced to rise up. Money value is influenced to reduce. Inflation may be influenced, due to global car consumers number increases, we would not have extra money to spend easily. Car expensive goods expenditure influences our spending habit to avoid to make car purchase decision more easily. So, human intellectual or foolish activities may bring inflation or deflation consequency in possible indirectly in macro economic view.

On conclusion, above pollution case explain that how and why human intellectual or foolish economic behaviors may bring inflation or deflation consequency as wll as economic growth or recession consequency as well as any goods demand and supply increasing or decreasing consequency. It implies that human behavior may have indirect relationship to influence any goods demand and supply number to either increase or decrease result as well as any goods price will be influenced to increase or decrease in micro and macro economic view.

9 798887 727585

Printed by Libri Plureos GmbH in Hamburg,
Germany